COMMUNICATION

COMMUNICATION

REDEEMING TALK TROUBLE

RICK THOMAS

COMMUNICATION:
Redeeming Talk Trouble

ISBN 978-1-966741-02-2

Rick Thomas

Edited by Sarah Hayhurst

Life Over Coffee
8595 Pelham Rd Ste 400 #406,
Greenville, SC 29615
LifeOverCoffee.com

No one has ever seen God; if we love one another, God
abides in us and his love is perfected in us.

(1 John 4:12)

For additional resources, visit
lifeovercoffee.com

Table of Contents

Dedication

Our Financial Partners,

You are the quiet ones who have made our work alive.
Only in heaven will you fully know how many people
were encouraged, motivated, taught, and changed by
our resources. Your belief in this work is personally
encouraging and globally transforming.

Thank you for your prayers and generous giving.
Through your sacrificial modeling of the gospel, we are
helping many people.

Foreword

Each counseling session regarding talk trouble problems begins similarly: "We have a communication problem." That is true in the most technical sense, though the couple's understanding of communication is nearly always limited and secularized. While they may not talk nicely to each other, the problem is much deeper than they realize. Communication problems begin in the heart of the person while reaching into the community of the Trinity. James asked, "What causes quarrels and conflicts?" and answered his question threefold by saying our passions, desires, and coveting ways are the source of a person's communication problems (James 4:1–2).

But communication is more than a heart problem; it is a divine problem. The Trinity is the original communicating community, and God made us in His image (Genesis 1:26–27). Though our hearts are broken and require a biblical rewire, it can only happen when we align our hearts to the divine—the original community. This book will walk you through how to do this. The first chapter will start where all good communication begins: with God. The second chapter will motivate you to branch out by exporting what you have learned to a close friend. I talk specifically about a husband leading his wife.

Finally, the third chapter will allow you to expand your communicative prowess to your more extensive group of friends. Perhaps the borders of redemptive communication will not stop with only these few relationships. The goal is that you will be able to build a genuine community with God, with yourself, with your closest friends, and with your extended group of friends. The most effective way to use this book is to read slowly, reflectively, and prayerfully while adding journaling and daily practice to your list of habits. I would not recommend reading just to be reading. At the end of each chapter, I have "call to action" opportunities to challenge you to work this content into your soul.

> Work out your own salvation with fear and trembling, for it is God who works in you, both to will and to work for his good pleasure
> (Philippians 2:12–13).

It would be best if you had a friend, spouse, or mentor that you could immediately share the content of this book. Finally, start communicating more effectively today to become a more effective communicator. Let the "call to action" opportunities work for you. Too often, books are read and shelved. I would not recommend you do that with this book. Your goal is not to notch your "book belt" as though you are on a quest to read books for the sake of reading.

May you aim to change. That may mean you read this book several times. Maybe it will become the source material among your friends. Perhaps you'll want to teach a class using this content or preach a sermon series. I appeal to you not to let the words in this book rest. Use them often. Please share them with others. I promise that your life and relationships will change if you practically grasp this content, measured by how well you talk to those closest to you.

That is my prayer for you and your friends.

—Rick

Let no corrupting talk come out of your mouths, but only such as is good for building up, as fits the occasion, that it may give grace to those who hear.

(Ephesians 4:29)

1

Perfect Communication

We are relational beings because God created us in His image (Genesis 1:26). God, who has always belonged to a Trinitarian community, made us in such a way that we desire to belong to a reciprocal community (Genesis 2:18). Made in the image of God means, in part, that we have similarities to God (James 3:9). One of the most intrinsic qualities that the Lord put into us is a desire to commune with others—those who are like us. The challenge, of course, is securing those trusted relationships where we can talk about the deeper and more meaningful things of life. There is a path forward.

Adam's Community

To want to relate to other people is God-like; it is imaging our Trinitarian God. A reason the Lord created Eve was so that Adam could more adequately reflect his Creator; it was not good for him not to have a companion (Genesis 2:18). Without an object to receive his love, Adam would not be able to know, experience, or emulate God entirely—God is love. It's like talking about ice cream versus tasting ice cream. Adam could understand love from his heavenly Father but could not fully experience it until he tasted it (Psalm 34:8)—until he could do what God was doing: loving another person (1 John 4:8). As they say, "You cannot understand a person until you walk a mile in their shoes."

Adam could not "walk a mile in the Lord's shoes" because he had no person like him to walk in similar paths. Adam's life would have a dead-end street feel without Eve. Our life would be the same if we were not communing within a human community. One of the most extreme expressions of this is solitary confinement. The Lord saw this problem and deemed it unsuitable for Adam to be alone, so He gave Adam a friend, a partner, someone for him to give as God had given him. For the first time in the history of the human race, Adam could live out a fuller reflection of his Creator by having an object for his affection.

Then we turn the page.

Along Came Sin

In Genesis chapter three, the author introduces sin through a walking, talking, stalking serpent. We know the story. Adam and Eve chose to sin, and from that point forward, every person born from them was selfish (Romans 5:12). The love Adam was supposed to give Eve turned onto himself. Eve reciprocated with a similar kind of self-centered love. Rather than seeing the other person as an opportunity to image God through others-centered soul care, our first two parents became self-serving. Adam and Eve replaced "esteeming others more than themselves" (Philippians 2:3–4) with esteeming themselves more than others, or what we call self-esteem today.

Selfishness is how sin transforms us into inverted, insatiable love cups. Knowing that selfish people could never save selfish people, the Father sent His others-centered Son to reverse the curse (Ephesians 2:1–10). The gospel—experienced through Christ—gives us an opportunity for a second birth (John 3:7), so we can be re-equipped, re-envisioned, and rerouted for how things should be. Even though the God-centered community was interrupted by the fall of Adam and Eve, the possibility of enjoying an others-centered community is available to anyone who wants it after they are born a second time.

True Community

The Father, Son, and Spirit are the purest iteration of this kind of reciprocating community. They are perfect *koinonia*. Nothing is more refined, exquisite, and profound than Father, Son, and Spirit, coequal and commingling. If you want to enjoy the most perfect human relationship possible, the Trinity has to be part of that relationship. Any human relationship without God is less than what it could be or should be. That is why non-Christians cannot have true koinonia. The Spirit will not inhabit the natural person (1 Corinthians 2:14). Paul hinted at this in Philippians 2:1 when he discussed participation in the Spirit. The word participation is the word koinonia or the word community.

> So if there is any encouragement in Christ, any comfort from love, any participation in the Spirit, any affection and sympathy, complete my joy by being of the same mind, having the same love, being in full accord and of one mind. Do nothing from selfish ambition or conceit, but in humility count others more significant than yourselves.
> (Philippians 2:1–3)

Biblical fellowship—participation in the Spirit or community—is sharing your most profound and personal relationship with another individual, which is your relationship with God.

– Rick Thomas

A husband and wife can relate to each other well and have many beautiful experiences together. Still, there will always be something missing in their relationship if they do not share their transparent and transcendent relationship with God—with each other. To have a real community with another human being, both persons must enter into mutual, reciprocating, and effective participation (fellowship) in the Spirit. Suppose they are not participating together with the Spirit of God. In that case, even if they have enjoyed every possible human experience, they will never fully experience the koinonia the Lord generously provides to any two (or more) people who want to participate with Him in that kind of community.

Unpacking Community

Think about the most potent and deep relationship you can have; it is with God. There is no other relationship better than what you have with the Lord. How could anything be better than the King of the universe, the Person who created and sustains you, communing with you? Suppose you want the most robust, profound, off-the-charts relationship with another human being. In that case, you must share your experience with your sovereign Creator, King—the Lord God Almighty with that individual.

If you do, you will share your greatest treasure with another (Matthew 6:21). Letting another person in on your treasure is the most vulnerable, intimate, profound, rich, transcending, honest, transparent, and complementary thing you could do for a relationship. The infographic helps to unpack what it means to have biblical fellowship with another person. Of course, real community—koinonia— applies to any friendship, e.g., if your small group of friends could do this, you would belong to one of the wealthiest groups in the world.

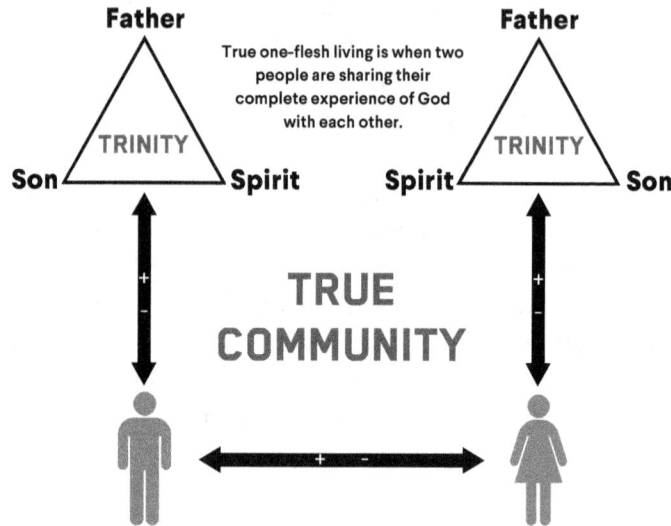

The person on the left could be anyone; I will call him Rick. The person on the right, we will call Lucia. You can see that Rick and Lucia have an individualized, independent, and personal relationship with God. Rick and Lucia enjoy the most profound relationship a person could ever want—God with them. They both are participating in the Spirit; the Lord has inhabited them. They are empowered, illuminated, encouraged, and motivated by God, and convicted and made to feel guilty when they sin against God (Proverbs 3:12; Hebrews 12:6). Rick and Lucia have a whole relationship with the Lord, which includes all their good and bad habits, all their good and bad days. They are doing things well in their walk with God (Ephesians 4:1), and there are things they have not fully matured into yet (Hebrews 5:12–14).

- **ON THE POSITIVE SIDE:** Rick and Lucia are appropriating the grace of God in their lives, and they are enjoying biblical success with God and each other (Joshua 1:8).

- **ON THE NEGATIVE SIDE:** Rick and Lucia are not appropriating the grace of God in all ways in their lives and the Spirit of God, which grieves and quenches Him at times (Ephesians 4:30; 1 Thessalonians 5:19).

Human Koinonia

Rick and Lucia are representatives of all Christians. You could say they have a light and a dark side (1 John 1:7–10) regarding their walk with the Lord. The right and wrong of their whole selves represent how they do community (koinonia) with the Lord. Though you must be a Christian to experience this kind of community, being a Christian does not automatically mean you have it. Being married and being a Christian does not always mean connecting and relating to your spouse at the deepest part of your personal experience, which is your intimate knowledge of and experience with God. You could "go to church" for years and never enjoy biblical fellowship with your spouse or any other person. That community requires a more profound amount of trust to engage another person in the deepest part of the soul.

And you would not give your most cherished treasure to someone you do not trust. If the person you share your deepest treasure with cannot steward the high honor of receiving your best prize, you must disqualify them from entering that experience with you—even if you're married to them. Regarding your relationship with the Lord, you may share part of your experience with Him with your spouse. You may let your spouse know some things you are learning or how you think about God and life. But if your spouse has a proven record of being unable to steward your deepest secrets, the more profound things will continue to be between you and the Lord. There is a level of koinonia you will not go to with your spouse or any other friend if they are not mature enough to handle the whole truth about you (John 16:12).

> There is therefore now no condemnation for those who are in Christ Jesus.
>
> (Romans 8:1)

You and I appreciate many things about the Lord, but probably nothing ranks higher than He does not condemn us. There is no more condemnation toward those who our Redeemer has saved. Our past, present, and future sins are under the blood of Christ, blotted out forever, and never held against us in any heavenly court of law. We have been justified, set free, and declared not guilty. As long as Christ lives, we will live in that freedom (Galatians 5:1). That truth has set us free (John 8:36). It sets us free to enter into His courts (Psalm 100:4), ready to share all of the thoughts and intentions of our hearts with Him, even though He already knows them (Hebrews 4:12–13). We do this because we are not afraid of Him. We are aware He is for us (Romans 8:31–39). We can be naked before God and not ashamed (Genesis 2:25). I am describing the kind of relationship every married couple should pursue with each other. That sort of koinonia will not happen quickly, but it's a lifetime of pressing into God and each other. Sharing the depths of our experience with God should be the goal for every couple.

One Thing Thou Lackest

It is typical when people come to me for counseling to discuss their communication problems. Communication comes from the Greek word koinonia. I do not think many (if any) understand that word's basic contours. They would be more discouraged if they fully understood the depth of their communication problems—as I have defined and explained here. What they are typically talking about and asking for is talk tips and some practical advice to help them communicate well with each other. I understand. They are trying to get along with each other, but they do not know how they are a million miles from what the Bible talks about when it talks about getting along with someone.

Christ did not come to help us to get along with each other. He came to transform us into Himself (1 John 3:8). In heaven, there will be perfect koinonia because there will be no sin. On earth, we must fight for this communication experience in relationships. There is a high price to enjoy "communal participation" in the Spirit. The biggest hindrance to koinonia is that we do not trust each other to handle the absolute truth about our lives. So, what do we do? We do not go there with them.

In the early part of our marriage, I remember how Lucia would share certain things with her friends—something she had not shared with me. I would become angry each time she did this. It was an insult. I would ask myself, "Why does she share her more intimate and personal thoughts with others but not with me?" My first response was to become upset with her. It took a while for me to realize how my jerk-ness was intimidating her from being intimate with me. It did not occur to me that she would not share because I was not mature enough to handle her truth. She knew she could share her more profound struggles with others, but she could not share those things with me because I was untrustworthy. Because of how I had responded to her in the past, she felt it would be wiser and safer not to let me into the deeper places of her heart. It takes a lot of courage to share struggles with someone else. It takes a lot of other-loving maturities to steward those more profound matters of the heart.

Call to Action

1. What is the meaning of koinonia?
2. Apart from imaging the Trinity, why is it vital to have at least one intimate, reciprocal relationship?
3. Are you currently experiencing real koinonia with your closest friend? If you are married, that friend should be your spouse.
4. If you are not, what is hindering you? (Make this question about you, not about the other person.) Key verses: Matthew 7:3–5.
5. What three practical things can you do to begin deeper participation with a friend? Perhaps sharing this resource with them will help envision and explain koinonia's essentialness.

2

Leading Your Wife In Koinonia

To fully release your vulnerable and intimate soul to another person, you must know the individual is trustworthy and will lovingly steward all of your inner truth. This quality in a marriage is one of a husband's most critical leadership requirements as he leads his wife in proper communication habits. We build our most vital and profound relationships upon trust, which is why we love God so much. Trust is why we share with Him our deepest and darkest thoughts; we know He will never condemn us (Romans 8:1). God provides a template for us to follow to break down communication barriers to enjoy the riches of intimate communication.

Building Trust

Trust is why we are okay with the Father's corrective care when we sin—we know He loves us (Hebrews 12:6). His corrections flow out of His unending and unstoppable love for us. This kind of love gives Him an all-access pass into our lives. He is the unique and perfect example to follow regarding relationship-making. He is the person we want to emulate. It took me a while to understand this regarding our marriage because I did not fully realize the importance of the "for us clause" in the gospel. In Romans 8:31, Paul asked, "If God is for us, who could be against us?" Then he explained what being "for us" meant as he doxologized about the gospel.

"He, who did not spare his own Son but gave him up for us all, how will he not also with him graciously give us all things?" (Romans 8:32). Do you see what Paul did? He connected how the Lord is for us to a practical outworking of the gospel. He said the Lord was for us, and Paul proved his point by reminding us that the Father sent His one and only Son to die on the cross to save us. If a person is willing to die for you, you can rest assured he is for you. He loves you inexhaustibly (John 15:13). And if he is for you to that degree, you know you can trust him—the essential requirement to release your vulnerable soul to someone fully.

This kind of gospel connection to our everyday lives is not what I demonstrated to my wife in the early years of our marriage. Though I was not a tyrant, and though we had many great times together, I was not fully and practically in tune with what it meant to be a gospelized man. Yes, I was for her because nobody else would dare to mess with her, but I was not for her in the way the Lord is for me. This gospel lack in my life gave her pause when sharing her innermost thoughts and struggles with me. I was not trustworthy to the degree I needed to be to release her from fear while inviting her to share with me in an open and vulnerable way. I had left just enough questions in her mind to make her wary of letting me fully into her world.

Without a Sin Plan

When we were dating, there was hardly a thing we did not discuss. It was open season for conversation, and all doors flung open as we shared our dreams and fears. The love flowed in those early days of dating. We had not known each other long enough to become disappointed or discouraged with each other. Sin was present but had not affected us enough to shut us down relationally.

That came later.

After we tied the knot and entered into a 24/7 relationship, the doctrine of sin became more of an issue. We were ignorant, two young people in love with no sin plan. Because we could not get away from each other, we could no longer keep our sinful ways masked from each other. Without training to wage war biblically, we waged war according to the flesh (2 Corinthians 10:3). Here are a few of our first fighting techniques—some of the tools you might find in any ungodly toolbox. Any of these characteristics create distance in a relationship, with no possibility of having biblical koinonia. To further complicate matters was my unwillingness to own the crimes I committed in the marriage.

This is where we were.

Accusing	Anger	Arrogance
Blame	Brooding	Condemnation
Criticalness	Excusing	Frustration
Grumbling	Guilt	Justification
Manipulation	No confession	Pouting
Rationalization	Selfishness	Self-righteous
Shame	Silence	Unforgiveness

Religious but Distant

On the surface, we "went to church." We were religious people in the proper sense of that word. We did ministry things. We prayed and read our Bibles each day. But there was a distance between us. We both had independent relationships with the Lord—relationships that did not intersect. It is possible to have made it to the end of our lives and still be together, still be in church, and still do ministry things in some way, shape, or form. I do not think those external activities would have changed much, even though our spiritual lives were like two ships passing in the night. There was no connection at the deepest and richest parts of our lives.

How sad when you cannot share your most treasured experience with the person you married: the Lord is a fantastic gift but not mutually enjoyed. Like a couple sitting in bed, playing video games on their own devices with people around the world, but not playing with each other. I shared my experience with God with friends, and Lucia shared her experience with God with friends, too, but we did not have a shared experience with God with each other. We could not connect at the soul level. The depth of our God-talk was about churchy things and churchy people. When it came to each other, we lived happily on the outside but spiritually lonely on the inside.

From Insult to Owning

Initially, I was offended that she would have spiritually intimate relationships with other people. As the Lord began to open my eyes, I began to see how I had set the tone for that kind of environment in our home. She did not shut down like that at the beginning of our relationship. Lucia was open with me and longed for me to lead her into more openness. Of course, I had no clue about such matters, so when she disappointed me, I responded with various forms of anger, i.e., harsh words, silent treatment, and accusations. Refer to the table again. I did not realize how my insensitivity perpetuated darkness in our home. Each unkind word was like a paper cut on her heart. Rather than owning my unkindness, I continued to wax on with my eye-for-an-eye responses to her (Matthew 7:3–5, 5:38–48).

Most Christian women want their husbands to love and lead them well (1 Peter 3:7). They want to be vulnerable (Ephesians 5:29). I have described it to many couples like a person walking up to you with their heart in their hands, reaching it out to give to you. Imagine standing there with another person's beating heart in your hands. That is the fragility we live before the Lord, knowing He could stomp us out in a moment. Yet we are willing to come before Him in that kind of vulnerability because we trust Him. A wife will never do that with her husband if he has a proven track record of not being entrusted with the high honor of stewarding her heart. That is what finally dawned on me. That is what I began to own. I had not created an environment of grace in our marriage. We were physically intimate. We loved each other. We continued to do a lot of fun things together, but there was a no-trespassing sign on her heart, and I was the one who put it there.

Step One: Step Up

Biblical fellowship is sharing your most profound and intimate relationship with another human, which is your relationship with God. *(Review the infographic on the next page)* There are two parts to your relationship with God— good and bad or light and dark. There are positive aspects in your life where you are appropriating the Lord's grace and living in the strength of His victory through the resurrection. There are other areas in your life where you have not yet applied the Lord's grace and are struggling. Biblical fellowship with another human being is when both people can share both sides of their experience with the Lord—the good and the bad. Trust is key to living in this kind of fellowship: "Can I trust you to steward my deepest vulnerabilities?" It became apparent that if I wanted to get into the deeper part of Lucia's soul, I needed to lead her by being vulnerable to her. I needed to step up to the plate and guide her in biblical koinonia rather than waiting for her to show me.

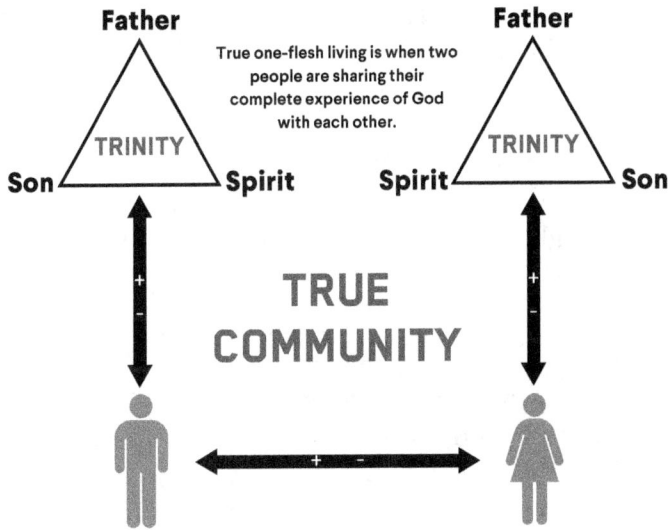

It was time to let her in on my dirty little secret: I was a failure as a husband. The irony is that she was well aware of my dirty little secret. The more significant obstacle was my unwillingness to own my failure, which only affirmed that she could not trust me. If a man is a thief but will not own his thievery, you know you cannot trust him. It is one thing to steal but to steal and not acknowledge your stealing makes you a person that others must be doubly cautious with when engaging. A person who will not own his sin has trustworthy issues, not to mention integrity, honesty, transparency, deception, self-righteousness, control, and discernment problems. Shall I go on with more reasons that caused Lucia to pause in her soul when opening up to me? As the leader of my home, it was my call as to whether I would make the first move. My overbearingness put her on her heels, and the empowering grace of God working through humility would begin to build the faith she needed to trust me again. In the past, I would wait for her to open up and own her sin. In those moments, I could fake humility while feeling smug, self-righteous, and grateful that she agreed. Think about how punishing that had to feel to her.

- Lucia sins.
- Lucia leads by owning her sin.
- I further condemn her through my arrogance and self-righteousness as I pontificate to her sin and how she needs to change.

Step Two: Live the Gospel

I honestly wanted Lucia to share her more profound thoughts about God, herself, life, and me. I did not want her only to find safety with others. It took me the longest time to realize I needed to lead her into it if that was what I wanted. Getting her to open up was not going to happen by verbally digging it out of her. Manipulating her through well-thought-out arguments, as though communication was a competitive event, would not work either. As for critique and shame? Forget about it. The radicality of the gospel cuts against the grain of prideful men. Here are a few examples that speak to that radicality:

- The way up is down (Philippians 2:1–11).
- The way in is out (Hebrews 13:13).
- The first will be the last (Matthew 20:16).
- Life comes through death (John 12:24).

- Man's wisdom is foolish, and God's foolishness is wisdom (1 Corinthians 1:18–25).
- To be strong, you must be weak (2 Corinthians 12:10).

If a man is going to lead his wife, he will have to learn how to serve her (Mark 10:45). If koinonia is the goal, open the door of your heart and invite her to your authentic self. Please give her a tour. Do a walk-through, articulating your failures, fears, and weaknesses. Let her see and experience your vulnerability.

Call to Action

Here are five questions you can share with your wife—a suggestive way for you to consider how to approach this type of communication in your marriage. If this kind of communication has not been the norm for you both, you may want to preface your questions with the following:

> Honey, if you ultimately knew I would not defend myself in any way or retaliate, how would you respond to the following things? You are free to answer however you want, and I will not defend myself, correct you, or try to manipulate you into my thinking. I also will not bring this conversation up in the future in a punitive way. I hope for you to experience the grace of God in your life, so it will release you to help me in areas where I have failed.

Do not say this if you don't mean it. The words are not a technique. If you have a change of heart and your words are true, here are a few biblical fellowship questions as you share your thoughts about yourself with your wife while drawing her out to give input. (Consider these questions your starter pack.)

1. What is one area of your life where you regularly fail and cannot gain victory? Talk to your wife about this area, leading her to a conversation while asking her for help.

2. What is one way you have failed her? Talk to her about this, seeking her forgiveness and asking how you can more effectively serve her.

3. What is a fear you have? Share that fear with your wife. You hold your heart in your hands while reaching it out for her loving stewardship.

4. Ask your wife to give her perspective on one of your blind spots—a thing you may not be able to see. Draw her out, appealing to her to help you see what you cannot see.

5. Ask your wife if she feels like you are for her (Romans 8:31). Draw her out, appealing to her to use specifics.

3

Building Dynamic Community

The most crucial relationship in your life is God. The most practical way to experience Him is in a community of like-minded believers who are intentional about helping each other mature in their relationships with Him. To know God better means your primary relationships should provide you with contexts to deepen your experience with Him (1 Corinthians 10:31). If your essential relationships do not give you that kind of care, you should consider changing your closest network of friends (Matthew 5:30; Hebrews 12:1). Knowing the Lord and experiencing Him with friends is the relational sweet spot for Christians.

Good Companions

Good friends are a biblical reason to pursue mature companions—those who want to motivate us to live God-glorifying lives (Hebrews 10:24–25). While it is true that bad companions can corrupt our morals (1 Corinthians 15:33), it is also true that good companions can make us better people. How would you respond to these questions as you think about your friendship list?

- Would you characterize your relationships as good or bad companions?
- Is your boyfriend (or girlfriend) a good companion?
- What about your spouse?
- How are your friends spurring you on to love and good works? If your closest relationships are not spurring you to love God more effectively, you should reconsider how you interact with them.

The What

The Lord becomes the *what*—the goal or aim—when building koinonia with others. He is *what* you want to become. Christ is the prize (Philippians 3:12-14). You hope to experience progressive change into Christlikeness (2 Corinthians 3:18), so you can enjoy a fuller experience with Him. What do you want to do? Experience the Lord in more profound ways. Establishing the Lord as the goal, you begin developing a methodology that will allow you to fulfill your call to walk in a manner worthy of His calling on your life (Ephesians 4:1-3, 5:1-2).

The How

The *how* aspect of building deeper with God and others makes the word koinonia an important word. It is the word for community, fellowship, and participation. (See other koinonia verses in Philippians 1:5, 2:1; 1 Corinthians 1:9; 1 John 1:3, 6-7.) To fully experience God, a community of like-minded people must be willing to participate in the Spirit for the cause of biblical fellowship. (See 1 Corinthians 12:27; Matthew 25:44-45.)

(Review the infographic on the next page.)

Knowing the Lord in all the ways you can know Him without body-to-body reciprocality is impossible. The "how" of community life is to build relationships with people who want to deepen their mutual experiences with the Lord and each other. With Christ as the goal for your community, you can now begin delving into the practical aspects of building and connecting your lives so you can experience that aim mutually. Here are seven suggestions to consider as you create a richer community life experience so you all can fully mature into Christlikeness.

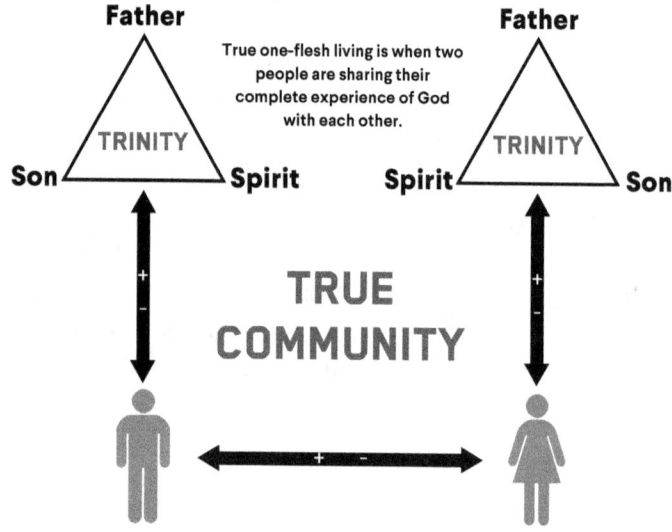

1: Establish Your Goal

I will not develop this any further than what I have already mentioned but will only reiterate the importance of making the Lord the prize for doing community life. If deepening your experience with God is not your chief purpose, your community will deteriorate into a social club. Suppose you think about your primary relationships in a "mission statement way." In that case, this could be your Community Mission Statement:

*We are here to deepen our relationship with the
Lord, which will happen in proportion to how we
deepen our relationship with each other.*

2: Understand Koinonia

Each person in your community will have to decide if
they will share their complete experience with God with
each other authentically. There are good and bad sides
to how they relate to God. For example, there are areas
in their lives where they are not appropriating the grace
of God, as evidenced by personal struggles and inter-
relational conflict. Nobody is perfect. Everyone is a work
in progress. Everybody in your group of close friends will
have sin problems and patterns in their lives. There are no
exceptions to this rule. It will be easier to share how they
are experiencing victory in Jesus, but it will be a struggle
for them to self-disclose in areas where they are not
experiencing biblical success.

The proportion in which every person in your
community is self-disclosing will be the proportion in which
your community will experience their most beneficial
possibilities with God. Nothing in group life will be more
challenging than living out this truth. It is impossible to
enjoy a complete expression of koinonia if your closest
friends are not willing to share their entire experience with
God. The same holds for you. Sharing half-truths about how
you are doing with the Lord will only allow others to enter
into half of your experience with the Lord—the safe side,
where you are living the dream. However, if you don't let
them into the darker side of your life, there is a good chance
you will always remain there.

3: Model Your Mission

Because you do not want to be naked and ashamed (Genesis 2:25), you cover yourself with fig leaves. That is what the Adamic people do. You carry a sense of fear, shame, and guilt and hope no one will expose you for who you are. The most effective way to motivate a person to share their complete experience with the Lord, specifically the darker side of themselves, is for you to share areas in which you struggle. You become the model for the person you want them to be. All good counselors know this truth. When someone comes to counseling, the counselee can easily (and wrongly) assume the counselor has his act together.

This presumption can intimidate the counselee and even hinder him from being self-disclosing. A wise counselor will want to diffuse this wrongheaded notion by letting the counselee know that he—the counselor—does not have it all together. There have been many times in counseling where I have shared my sin struggles. In doing so, I hope to release the person from fear of being transparent. Trying to hide your sin is as futile as hiding your skin color. The quicker you can get over yourself, the faster you can access one of the most effective means of grace given to you: the body of Christ. A wise, humble, community-minded person will openly discuss the good and bad sides of his relationship with the Lord.

4: Build Trust

The thing that will hinder you from openly sharing the darker things in your life is trust. Usually, trust issues revolve around two critical questions: Can I trust you? How will you respond to me after I reveal the real me? For example, Will you judge me? Will you make fun of me? Will you critique me or gossip about me? Are you competent enough to help me? If I share my struggles with you, can you help me? This relational tension is where you must be patient with people (1 Thessalonians 5:14). It can take years for someone to open up. Sanctification may sound nice on paper, but things can become quite complicated when you put a bunch of messed up people in a room together.

5: Enjoy Small Talk

Small talk leads to deep talk. Typically, launching into deep conversations with people you do not know is unwise. It is even more foolish to pull things out of people—those uncomfortable with that kind of intrusive conversation. They may want help at some level but must come to you on their terms, not yours. Because of the tentativeness of people, it will be vital for you to learn the value of small talk. Love your friends while encouraging and building trust. Do not expect in six weeks of relationship building with a friend what you have learned in twenty years of walking with the Lord. Give it time. You keep on modeling your mission. Let them see your freedom in Christ (Galatians 5:1). Let them see your example of how to reveal the darker side of life while teaching them how to appropriate the grace of God in those areas of struggle.

6: Value Intentionality

It will be easy to lose purpose with your friends, which makes being intentional essential. The gospel-centered life comes with a cross. The temptation to be less authentic and more shallow speaks to the essentialness of keeping your eye on the goal (Hebrews 12:2). Jesus never lost sight of His purpose. There was "joy set before Him," which motivated Him to endure the process of redeeming hurting, lost, and enslaved people (Hebrews 2:14–15; Matthew 26:38–39). Intentional community building invariably leads to conflict, so people default to superficial community life. It is too hard, and we can be too stubborn.

7: Create Contexts

Because of the challenge of getting people to open up and the time involved in building trust with them, it would be wise to have several contexts where you connect with your community. Let them experience you in different settings, doing other things. Traditionally, we have used six different environments where we sought to do life with our friends. We did not want our weekly small group gathering to be the only opportunity to build with our folks relationally.

CHURCH CONSTRUCT

ONE MONTH

Church Meetings

Small Group

Coffee

Dinner

Email

Ministering

Events

OUR LIVES

- **CORPORATE MEETING:** Lucia and I would typically connect with our friends each Sunday morning at our church meeting. These are mostly fun and light conversation times, though praying and more severe discussions happen, too.
- **SMALL GROUP MEETING:** We did life together in a smaller group setting throughout the year. This context was our small group meeting.
- **COUPLE'S MEETINGS:** We tried to have each couple

over to our home at least once a month. These meetings proved to be excellent contexts to build with them more privately. These meetings enhanced our weekly group meetings. Historically, we blocked out each Thursday evening of the month for these times of fellowship.

- **MEN:** I would meet with the men in our small community once a month to talk more personally about life and God.
- **EVENTS:** We did all kinds of fun things together.
- **SOCIAL MEDIA:** We regularly communicated with each other through different types of social media.

Tying It Together

With these contexts in mind, there are also five means of grace taught from Scripture about how change happens. You may use these means with any of the previously mentioned strategies. These means are not in any particular order and are not equally applied. It depends on the person, the time, and the need of the moment as to what means is most helpful in a person's life. Here are those means of grace—five ways change happens:

- God will change you.
- The Bible will change you.
- There is a requirement for you to change yourself.
- The Lord will use situations to change you (Genesis 50:20).
- There is a call to the body of Christ to serve the body of Christ in the change process.

Call to Action

I have two sets of questions for you. The first set helps you examine your heart regarding biblical fellowship (koinonia). I appeal to you to spend time with the Lord, discussing your thoughts about living in a community with other believers. It would be helpful to share your thoughts with someone close to you. I also recommend you have a solid understanding of the previous two chapters to help you better handle authentic community. Reviewing those chapters can make community life an incredible means of grace, especially if the group comes together with a desire to mature in their sanctification.

1. What are the risks of not having biblical fellowship?
2. How close should someone get to you?
3. How honest should you be with others?
4. How close should you pursue the opposite sex in biblical fellowship?
5. What does koinonia look like practically at work, home, with roommates, dating, marriage, and non-Christian environments?
6. Can you fellowship at the same level as married people if you are single?
7. Can you have fellowship the same way with all Christians, including your Christian relatives?
8. What hinders biblical fellowship for you?

This second set of questions are the ones Lucia and I regularly ask each other. They always get the ball rolling conversationally as we transparently share our experiences with God—the good and the bad—with each other.

1. What is the Lord doing in your life?
2. What has the Lord taught you lately?

3. How have you applied what He taught you to your life?
4. Will you help me in this "specific" area of temptation?
5. What have you read or heard that is helping you in your sanctification?
6. How is the grace of God working in a particular area of sin?
7. What specific areas are you struggling with now?
8. How can I serve you in a particular area of your sanctification?
9. What are some ways in which you are leading your friends?
10. How are you applying the sermon from this past Sunday?

4

Summing It Up

Thank you for reading this communication book. You can now see what I said in the Foreword: "Communication problems begin in the heart of the person while reaching into the community of the Trinity." If you want to transport your talk trouble to redemptive communication, it will be one of the hardest things you will ever do, though it will be one of the most rewarding. God favors the humble (James 4:6) but will oppose the proud.

Your greatest ally in this journey is the Lord. Ask Him to give you favor in proportion to your willingness to humble yourself before Him and your friends. If you do this, expect good things. He is for you. Now go to a trusted friend and start talking about the content in this book. Practice leads to maturity. The teacher will learn more than the student.

> For though by this time you ought to be teachers, you need someone to teach you again the basic principles of the oracles of God. You need milk, not solid food, for everyone who lives on milk is unskilled in the word of righteousness, since he is a child. But solid food is for the mature, for those who have their powers of discernment trained by constant practice to distinguish good from evil.
>
> (Hebrews 5:12–14)

May We Help?

If we can serve you, please visit our coffee shop at lifeovercoffee.com. Our super-sized cyber home is accessible from anywhere worldwide as long as there is the Internet. Our goal is to come alongside you to help envision you as you engage our resources for equipping so you can export what you are learning to others for the exaltation of Christ in your life and theirs.

> What you have heard from me in the presence of many witnesses entrust to faithful men who will be able to teach others also.
>
> (2 Timothy 2:2)

The most effective way you can accomplish these admirable goals is through the daily reflection of our resources over an extended period. Let these gospel-centered truths settle into your soul. With time, patience, and diligence, you can experience a long-term, satisfying, and effective change. Personal change does not happen quickly, but it does happen. It will require perseverance on your part. A few weeks in our "coffee shop" has proven practically transformative to many people.

What Others Say

"I'm not sure how I ran into your site, but I'm so glad I did. You inspire me to serve our LORD and to want to follow closely after His desire for my life. I can see your gift to help an abundance of people to find paths in this life to shine brightly for God's glory. Thank you for sharing, and God bless you."

– Sharyon

"Thank you for all your hard work producing these podcasts and articles. Your work has truly changed my life."

– Darren

"I recently learned about your ministry and website from a friend. And I have told my friends as well. Your work is brilliant. I'm grateful for you and appreciate you more than you will ever know. I will remember you in prayer regularly. May God richly bless you and yours always. Thank you!"

– Kim

"For several years, I have read your articles and printed them off to give to those I counsel in my church. I have been helped personally in many ways and appreciate how relevant the articles are to so many people's situations. The webinars are beneficial! Thank you."

– Barbara

About the Author

 Rick Thomas launched the Life Over Coffee global training network in 2008 to bring hope and help for you and others by creating resources that spark conversations for transformation. His primary responsibilities are resource creation and leadership development, which he does through speaking, writing, podcasting, and educating. In 1990 he earned a BA in Theology and, in 1991, a BS in Education. In 1993, he received his ordination into Christian ministry, and in 2000, he graduated with an MA in Counseling from The Master's University. In 2006, he was recognized as a Fellow of the Association of Certified Biblical Counselors (ACBC).

Other Books Available from
Life Over Coffee

Boasting in Weakness
Centering Your Marriage on Christ
Communication
Complete Marriage
Don't Apologize
Exchange the Truth for a Lie
Help My Marriage Has Grown Cold
Identity Crisis
Local Church
Loving Me
Mad
Marriage Devotion We Are One
Politics and Culture
Parenting Devotion from Zero to Adulthood
Sex, Temptation, and Modesty
Storm Hurler
The Cyber Effect
The Talk
Wives Leading
You Decide